So...
You want to be a
Doctor?

Dr David Hopkins

KOGAN PAGE

YOURS TO HAVE AND TO HOLD
BUT NOT TO COPY

First published in 1998

Apart from any fair dealing for the purposes of research or private study, or criticism or review, as permitted under the Copyright, Designs and Patents Act 1988, this publication may only be reproduced, stored or transmitted, in any form or by any means, with the prior permission in writing of the publishers, or in the case of reprographic reproduction in accordance with the terms and licences issued by the CLA. Enquiries concerning reproduction outside those terms should be sent to the publishers at the undermentioned address:

Kogan Page Limited
120 Pentonville Road
London N1 9JN

© David Hopkins, 1998

The right of David Hopkins to be identified as author of this work has been asserted by him in accordance with the Copyright, Designs and Patents Act 1988.

British Library Cataloguing in Publication Data

A CIP record for this book is available from the British Library.

ISBN 0 7494 2786 8

Typeset by JS Typesetting, Wellingborough, Northants.
Printed in England by Clays Ltd, St Ives plc.

Contents

Acknowledgements iv

Introduction 1

1 So you want to be a doctor? 3

2 What is being a medical student like? 10

3 What happens in your houseman's year? 15

4 What happens in the senior house officer years? 23

5 What are the registrar years like? 33

6 What is it like being a GP? 46

7 What is being a consultant like? 52

8 What is it like being a woman in medicine? 57

9 What are the financial aspects of being a doctor? 63

10 Are there other options within medicine? 73

11 Decision time 75

Acknowledgements

I owe a great debt of thanks to the many colleagues and friends who have proof-read the various chapters for their advice and support. In particular, Dr Beth de Sousa for her contribution of the chapter concerning women in medicine, and Victoria Cumming for the loan of a typewriter!

Finally, I owe greatest thanks to my parents for supporting me through medical school, feeding me when I was hungry, teaching me how to iron and generally being there.

Introduction

Every year, thousands of school and college hopefuls sit their 'A' levels in the hope of reaching the grades required to get into medical school. Ten years ago, I was one of them, and by some bizarre twist of fate, fortune and a fair bit of hard work, I made it.

What I had very little appreciation of was exactly what I'd made it into. My mind was full of all sorts of impressions, gained mostly from favourite television shows. However, inevitably these were dramatized to show the same amount of excitement in half an hour that most doctors see in a month, while leaving out all the less exciting elements of medical life.

I'd done a bit of research, including talking to the careers advisers at school, and had even done one of those 'discover your right career' questionnaires that seem to take into account everything from your shoe size to your favourite colour! I spent a day in theatre with a local surgeon who demonstrated the finer aspects of varicose vein stripping to me before I had to leave due to a peculiar light-headed feeling, and I had a quick chat with a local GP who gave an 'in my day' talk before going off to do his visits. My father was a high street pharmacist and my sister is a dentist, so family advice was available. Despite all this, I still maintain that, on reflection, I had no real idea of what I was getting myself into.

Nor, as it transpired, did many of my friends at medical school. Being a doctor, we were to discover, isn't just about medicine and making people better, it is about a way of life, a career-dominating existence, and a whole lot more besides.

Some of my friends dropped out of medical school very early on. Others left in the second, third, even fourth years of the five-year course as they realized that this wasn't for them. Current national estimates are that it costs nearly £200,000 to train each doctor, but that between 7 and 12 per cent will fail to complete their course at medical school, and that 5 years after qualifying a further 7 per cent have dropped out. Furthermore, it is a terrible financial burden on the students themselves. It costs a lot of money to be at university now, especially with the inevitable introduction of annual fees.

To me this seems a terrible waste of people's time and of national resources. This country is desperately short of doctors. General practice is in something of a crisis, with shortages of new GPs and the early retirement of older ones. Hospital posts are being propped up by the employment of doctors from other countries, especially Germany and South Africa.

So, what's the purpose of this book?

This is a relatively short book, designed to give people interested in medicine an insight into what lies ahead – the training, work and lifestyle. In particular, this book is for pupils at school or college from GCSE upwards who are seriously interested in medicine as a career, and their parents who may want to have an idea themselves of what it is all about, so that they can discuss it further with their son or daughter, giving constructive advice. I have deliberately tried to keep things brief, constructive and informative. I have tended to write about my own personal observations and opinions expressed by colleagues to me over the last year rather than facts and figures, which tend to be rather boring and fail hopelessly to convey any real meaning.

Finally, if you are thinking about medicine as a career, and think you know it all already, then I'll pose you a question. I am 27 years old, went to medical school aged 18 and didn't have to resit any years. So, how long have I been qualified, what is my likely hospital rank and how much longer have I got to go before I'm a consultant or GP?

If you can answer that, then you've already got an idea of what lies ahead, but if you're a bit unsure, then you'd better read on!

1

So you want to be a doctor?

I still find it hard to believe that I was ever accepted into medical school. It was 1988, I was in the first few months of my gap year and I had an interview at Southampton University Medical School. Intriguingly, the members of its rugby team are known as the 'moose men' and wear fake antlers on their heads on particularly drunken Saturday nights in local pubs in some bizarre, inexplicable belief that this makes them more attractive to the opposite sex. Even more bizarre is the fact that it seems to work, but we'll talk about medics' social lives later.

'So why do you want to be a doctor?' asked one of my interviewers. I believe he was the Pre-clinical Dean of Medicine – an important man who could single-handedly decide my medical destiny. Not an unreasonable question either, given the circumstances.

'I want to be able to spend my life helping people and doing good to people in need'

came my stuttering reply. I'd practised that one.

'So why not a priest or a nurse or a policeman?'

I think he'd played this game before. I also got the impression I could lose this game badly.

'Well, you see, I've just always wanted to be a doctor. It all stems from when I was ill in hospital as a child and a doctor saved my life . . . I've been full of admiration ever since – I'd love to be able to do that too.'

Two weeks later, a letter came through the post saying I'd been accepted. Either the Pre-clinical Dean had believed me or he'd seen through my story. Either way, it would transpire, in my interview I'd readily displayed the ability to bluff while looking at someone straight in the eye. As all honest doctors will tell you, this is one of the most important skills of all for a doctor to master, and is probably why I was accepted.

Getting into medical school

I am afraid to say, however, that the basic fact is that to get into medical school remains very difficult, and for every one place on offer in this country, there will be at least half a dozen to a dozen applicants. In other words, you've got to be better than the other 12 out there to get in. So, how do you do this?

Exams

First, the GCSE results are important, as that's the only pre-'A' level academic information that medical schools have to go on. Think straight 'A's and you're probably on the right wavelength. However, recent research has suggested that an ability to cram for school exams and achieve high grades is not necessarily a useful skill or requirement for being a good doctor. So, now, non-academic factors are also considered – being a school prefect, sports superstar, artistically gifted, something, anything, that suggests you are able to maintain a high academic level while also having time and energy to pursue other interests.

Which 'A' levels?

'A' level choices are important, but which ones you do should be a joint decision between yourself and your school. The most important thing is to get high grades, as low grades don't look good. Traditionalists would recommend doing the three sciences, but you don't have to. Having said this, chemistry is probably vital as so much of the early medical school training has a biochemical and physiological basis. I did biology as well and found that a very useful companion – indeed, friends at medical school who hadn't done biology 'A' level found themselves working harder to keep up. Physics is an odd one. I didn't do it for several reasons, but mainly because I didn't enjoy it and didn't think I'd get a good grade in it. I never missed it as a medical student. I did maths instead and got an A grade, my only A. Although maths isn't wholly relevant to medicine, the grade was part of the reason for my being offered a place.

On reflection, I wish I'd done something more interesting for my third choice, like French, but I was advised against it at the time. In your own case, it will be up to you to agree with your teachers what subjects you will enjoy and do well in, and which will be appropriate for medical school. If in doubt, ring up your first choice of medical school and ask what they like to have from their applicants.

Other qualifications

Finally, it is wise to have attempted to gain a bit of work experience. There are several reasons for this. First, as a result you may realize that, despite it being your childhood ambition to become a doctor, medicine isn't actually what you want to do. Second, it sounds good at your interview to say that you've spent some time working in a doctor's surgery or hospital. Third, you may learn something from the people you work with about the career first-hand.

To get experience, use a bit of initiative, and contact your local GP or hospital, spend some holiday time doing voluntary work in a hospital or send some letters to local surgeons asking if you can watch an operating list one day. You may get a good result, you may not, but at least you can say you tried.

> **Tips for getting into medical school**
>
> - Try to get some practical experience beforehand.
> - Choose your 'A' levels with care, get advice from your teachers and aim to spend two years studying a subject you enjoy, will do well in and which is relevant to medicine.
> - Non-academic achievements can be as important as the academic, so try to be 'interesting'.
> - Think the whole thing through carefully, then go for it!

Where to apply to

Well, there are three traditional groupings:

- Oxford and Cambridge
- London medical schools – Guy's, George's and so on
- university medical schools – Southampton, Nottingham, Bristol, Cardiff, Belfast and others.

Where you choose to go will determine not only your geographical location for the next five years, but also, to a degree, the style of your medical teaching, the sorts of friends you will have the opportunity to make and the size of your overdraft at the end of the course.

Oxford and Cambridge

First, if you are academically brilliant, fancy sitting an extra set of Oxbridge entrance exams and have a strong calling for tradition, then Oxford or Cambridge may be for you. There is little doubt as to the beauty of these cities or to their historical meaning and international value.

If Oxford or Cambridge is what you want, then you are likely to know this already – you can probably feel it in your bones that this is where you're meant to be and you are probably in the absolute top level of all your classes at school. However, despite the high selection criteria and historical strength, to assume that the training is better than that received at other medical schools is questionable. Indeed, many would now say that the modern, purpose-built facilities and futuristic thinking of other universities provide students with a better service.

Bear in mind also that if you are successful in getting a place, you may not actually spend your entire five years at Oxford or Cambridge. Come the clinical years, when hospital experience becomes key, many Oxford and Cambridge medical students end up in London or other cities where the hospital experience is more available.

London medical schools

The London medical schools are all impressive places in their own rights, provide excellent teaching and friends who've been there for their training overflow with stories of fun and excitement. They are all different from each other and there is keen inter-hospital rivalry, especially in sports. Teaching styles differ as well and, indeed, one senior consultant with whom I have worked says he can tell which London medical school a doctor has trained at purely from the way they hold a tendon hammer! London is huge, dynamic and exciting, so that in itself is an attraction for some.

The only minus point of London when compared with other medical schools is the cost of living there. Let's face it, medicine is, at a minimum, a five-year course, six if you include a BSc (an extra element to the degree), and, if you fail a year, every extra year means extra debt. London is wickedly expensive to live in, with everything from the cost of a pint of lager to renting a room costing over the national average. Compare, for example, the cost of renting a room in a student house in London with one in Southampton, Nottingham or Cardiff. In London it'll be £50, while in the other cities you would expect to pay £35 per week for an equivalent size and location. A drink in a pub may cost £2.00 in London, £1.50 in the other cities. Then there's the cost of food, clothing, public transport, taxis, nightclubs .... It all adds up and has to be paid off somehow, later on.

University medical schools

The third option is to choose one of the non-Oxbridge university medical schools. There are lots to choose from now, and all are well respected throughout the medical world. I chose Southampton because it was far enough away from home (south-west London) to give me my own space, while still being within easy distance of family for when I wanted to go back for a weekend. Others chose Southampton for its access to the coast and enviable windsurfing possibilities, and so on. Newcastle has great football and rugby teams locally, Nottingham has the National water sports centre (and, of course, the forest). Everyone has their own reasons for being drawn to any place or, ultimately, it may come down to the simple fact of which ones offer an interview.

The university medical schools may not have the long history of Oxbridge and London, but I can still think of several reasons for going to a university-based medical school.

- You'll spend at least your first three years in the company of non-medics (that is, people studying other subjects, such as English, engineering, geography, education and so on). This gives you the opportunity to develop a healthy variety of friends, which will be of immense value to you in years to come. There is nothing more potentially boring than a doctor who has only medical friends. It makes for an insular lifestyle, dull work-orientated dinner party conversations and breeds arrogance through ignorance of other people's lifestyles. In my time at medical school, I made friends with people doing education, law, engineering, geography and other degrees. Five years on, these people are still some of my best friends and, just when I think my head is going to explode with medical overload, it's great to spend a weekend or holiday with them and be able to leave it behind completely.
- Teaching standards are excellent, with many universities providing modern, purpose-built facilities for lectures, dissection rooms, videos, laboratories and so forth. Universities have the ability to provide medical students with the best of both worlds – the campus facilities, sports, clubs, grounds and the social network that all come with being a part of a modern university as well as

the best of up-to-date educational facilities required for not only medicine but also the other degrees, such as biology, physiology, the sciences.
- The financial implications, as stated previously.

Summary

- The first hurdle on the medical steeplechase is to get into medical school.
- Good GCSE results are the norm.
- Good 'A' level results are especially important, but discuss which subjects to do carefully with advisers and contact your first-choice medical school to see if your choices are acceptable – doing three sciences is not a necessity.
- Maintain a variety of non-academic interests, be they sports, hobbies or other things.
- Use your initiative to try and gain work experience.
- Don't just go for any old medical school – consider your options carefully and the implications of your choice, including the financial aspects, the people you are likely to meet and the style of training. Think about what you would prefer.
- If you figure medicine is for you, then give it your best shot, go for it and good luck.

2

What is being a medical student like?

The extra-curricular activities

Freshers' week at university. If you've got this far, then you've already done pretty well. You've jumped the opening hurdles of the medical steeplechase and are probably feeling fresh and excited, and you need a jockey on your back like never before to keep you under control. Unfortunately Mum and Dad are miles away, so you'll probably be completely out of control, swerving everywhere and deliberately bumping into the particularly attractive members of the opposite sex. All students, no matter which medical school they are at, seem to have fun – it's part of being a student!

Medics, in fact, are renowned for always going just that extra step further. If there's ever a party worth going to, it'll be at one of the medical student's houses. Indeed, I remember a film that was advertised with the phrase 'Be afraid, be very afraid' and I'm sure this was inspired by the producer accidentally stumbling in to a medics' party and witnessing only previously dreamt of horrors!

Parents and faint-hearted people, do not fear – this is all a subtle part of the training for the life that lies ahead. Indeed, I distinctly remember the first few months of my first job as a junior doctor. I was working around 86 hours a week, but somehow felt it was easier than being a student! Being a student is about learning and passing exams while stretching yourself to the furthest physical and mental limits possible. As a result, when you finally qualify as a doctor, you know your limits. When faced with needing to stay up all night without any sleep to keep a patient alive you know you can do it because you've stayed up all night so many times as a student!

Medical school is very hard work combined with great fun. For example, when I was at school, we used to have, say, 35 hours of lessons per week, plus homework, sport and exams. When I went to medical school, I had a similar number of lectures per week, I had homework (now called project work), I still did sport (except the rugby wasn't against schoolboys but the local police force, who hit hard and drank heavily afterwards) and there were still exams (which got tougher and tougher). Added to the agenda was an awful lot of partying and alcohol, with at least a couple of nights a week of not going to bed before seeing the milkman do his rounds. Then there was the part-time work that I, like a lot of students, had to do to keep financially afloat (I used to do night shifts at the local Mr Kipling factory, which really did bake exceedingly good cakes). You may now be starting to appreciate why I said earlier that working as a junior doctor actually seemed easier than being a student.

Not surprisingly, all this socializing and work takes its toll, normally on what most civilized human beings would consider to be essential daily requisites. After my first term at medical school, I felt exhausted, starved and overdrawn. Going back to the family in holidays became something of a necessity – an opportunity to eat food again, wash all my clothes and catch up on sleep. Such is student life!

Money – or lack of it

In practice, there are other elements to university life that are really the controlling factors. Money rapidly disappears with heavy socializing and so how much you have controls how much fun you can afford – especially where alcohol is concerned. You can't buy a pint if you've no money in your pocket. Most students do extra jobs during term time, including bar work, auxiliary nursing work, factory work, even taking part in medical experiments. Holidays are for extensive amounts of project work while also doing temping jobs nearer home. As mentioned earlier, I did night shifts in a factory, and, during holidays, washed dishes in a local cafe, drove a lorry in London and worked in a timber yard. All good fun on a short-term basis and the money certainly helped pay for the fun during term time.

Making the grade

Medical school will challenge you with exams and new learning expectations that make 'A' levels seem like a walk in the park. Whereas previously you may have been in the top 10 per cent of your school academically for most of your life (and will have been getting A and B grades at school as the norm), when you reach medical school, everyone has this same high level of intelligence. Therefore, the competition hots up, so you will get Es and Fs if you don't put the work in. Something like 30 people in my year had to come back in the middle of the summer holidays to resit exams, after which some of them were thrown out for good. Not the best way to spend the summer, and may I humbly suggest to any budding students that falling behind can lead to disaster.

What medical students do

- An option is offered by almost all medical schools to do an additional year for a BSc.
- Learning is by a combination of book work, lectures, research, lab. work and, most importantly, hospital ward work, ward rounds, teaching sessions with doctors and sessions sitting in with GPs. This is traditionally split into pre-clinical and clinical years, although many medical schools are now mixing the two together.
- The aim is to gain a sound knowledge of the anatomical, physiological and pathological processes involved in patients

- illnesses and treatments, while developing interaction skills for dealing with patients and relatives.
- The skills required to do basic practical procedures are also established – taking blood, inserting drips, taking proper medical histories from patients, learning how to examine them and recognize physical signs of disease.
- During the last few years of the course, most medical schools give students opportunities to work in a variety of hospitals, in a variety of specialities, to allow them to broaden their knowledge of the specialities and how different hospitals work.
- All medical schools also allow a period of time known as the 'elective', which is when the students can choose a place pretty much anywhere in the world where they go to work for a few months. Officially, the aim of this is to gain knowledge of other countries' medical systems, but, unofficially, it is to have a decent holiday. I went to Thailand and had a really good time, some friends went to Australia and others even got to go to Bermuda.
- After five years, you sit finals to gain a medical degree. Passing these exams essentially means that you are fit to work as a doctor, but only under supervision, until a full year of working as a doctor has been completed. This is known as the pre-registration house year, after which you will be formally registered with the General Medical Council (the governing body of the profession) as a registered doctor.

If you are now having doubts

Some or all of this may sound rather daunting, even frightening, when you are considering medicine as a career. All I can say is that if I had known this when I was still at school, then I would probably have felt quite daunted by it as well. However, when you are actually going through it, it's all quite exciting. Everything happens gradually and carefully. The schools pretty much take you by the hand and lead you to where you need to go. There are personal tutors keeping a close eye on how you're doing – academically and personally – and you'll have friends all around to support you in times of worry.

Medical school is exactly what you make of it, and no matter which one you go to or who you meet or what you get up to, I'm sure you'll enjoy it. No doubt you'll make the odd mistake along the way, but don't we all?

If you want more information on how to survive uni, there are lots of books now giving 'essential' student survival tips, but if I were you, I'd just get out there and work it out for yourself.

Summary

- It's as much fun as you want it to be.
- It lasts a minimum of five years.
- You'll make some great, life-long friends.
- You'll have to pass some really tough exams, but with a bit of work you'll manage OK.
- Don't fall behind with the work – it's a nightmare catching up.
- Keep a close eye on your finances and be prepared to do part-time and holiday jobs.
- Use your free time at medical school to adventure into things you've never done before, be it sports, clubs, societies or whatever takes your fancy.
- All I can say is, trust in the system – do the work, sit the exams, have some fun and, before you know it, you'll be a qualified doctor!

3

What happens in your houseman's year?

Getting accurate information about what it's like

If you are thinking about a career in medicine or just want to know more about what being a doctor is all about, then your initial problem will be in finding appropriate sources of information.

First, there are all the television programmes about medicine – so many that I can't really believe the public's appetite is big enough to cope. Television programmes are always dramatized, rarely factually correct, never show the whole picture and are often politically biased. Furthermore, they almost always concentrate on life within a hospital or GP's surgery, rarely depicting a doctor's life outside of work.

Probably the most popular series recently among junior doctors was *Cardiac Arrest* with Helen Baxendale on BBC 1. It had, without doubt, the most twisted and corrupt storylines I can recall, and the programme was widely considered worth watching purely for Helen herself, but, alas, it wasn't a particularly accurate reflection of day-to-day goings on.

The next most likely source of information as to what being a doctor is all about is a real one. We doctors love being asked about our lives, mainly because we see ourselves as being the self-sacrificing victims of a stingy beaurocracy. Younger doctors are too busy to stop and talk, however, and older doctors will invariably offer prized words of wisdom and summarize life as a doctor in a couple of brief sentences. These normally start with the immortal words 'Well, in my day...' and finish with 'These young doctors don't realize how easy it is for them nowadays'. Great if you want a history lesson, but otherwise not the best of information to base a career decision on.

So, what's the bottom line? What's it really like? How will my life be affected by a simple career choice?

Profile of a typical junior doctor

Well, the chances are that a typical junior doctor will have left school/college at the age of 17 or 18. They will have enjoyed many years of success at school and probably never failed an exam in their life. They may well have taken a gap year. They will then have spent a minimum of five years at medical school, been shocked to discover that exam failure isn't just something that happens to other people, and will now be proudly pinning that first 'Dr...' badge on to their white coat at the tender age of 24. Day one as a working, earning doctor is about to begin.

How things might otherwise have turned out

This age bit is actually quite a significant thing to think about. If, for example, you'd left school aged 16 to become an apprentice car mechanic, say, you would, by this stage, have been earning an income for 8 years. So when, as a newly qualified doctor, you turn up for work driving your clapped out Skoda and someone with half your educational training whizzes past you in a new Golf GTi, you could be forgiven for scratching your head in a quizzical way and wondering where the justice in all this is. 'Justice' probably won't come your way for another ten years, when you will have paid off all your student debts and you'll be on triple that person's income, but when you're just starting out, it does seem a rather long time to wait.

You could, on the other hand, have decided to go to university to do a really useful three-year degree in something like Greek mythology or landscape architecture. You would probably have had about 10 hours' lectures a week (rather than 35) for just 3 years before leaving at the age of 22 to join a managerial training scheme with a top travel agency, building society or high street chain, earning around £15,000 a year straight away for a 40-hour week. Equally, you could have done a law degree, have left university, nearly completed a two-year training contract with a law firm and be looking to start as a solicitor in a London firm on over £20,000 a year.

How things have turned out

You did not do any of these things. Instead, you are a newly qualified doctor. Your first year as a doctor, as mentioned earlier, is called the 'houseman's year'. Your official title is a pre-registration house officer. Americans would call you an 'intern', and grumpy senior sisters will just call you useless. You will have a daunting overdraft (see Chapter 9) and butterflies in your stomach! All of this, however, falls away behind you as you start your career.

The implications of graduation

Your first and most important act as a new doctor is not to go on a ward round, but to ring up your bank and demand a new cheque guarantee card, Visa card and just about anything else you can think of with the title 'Dr' proudly emblazoned on it.

Meanwhile, you will also be struggling to cope with the totally overwhelming pride of everyone in the family, from Gran to the pet dog, that you are now finally a doctor. This, however, must be set in context as, for the last five years, your Gran had to reluctantly admit to her friends that, yes, you were one of those strange, untidy student things. All of a sudden, you are now a respectable member of society she can invite round when she has friends over!

Your final satisfaction will come from all the 'lay' people around you believing that you are actually already something between a consultant and God himself in terms of medical knowledge. You will immediately be expected by friends and relatives alike to wish desperately to stop at the scene of any road traffic accident so that you can perform some lifesaving heroics on a poor victim and be able to offer valued opinions over lunch on triple artery bypass grafting and the latest genetic testing for CJD.

Even more amazing is the sudden realization that, even though you actually don't have a clue what you're talking about, everyone around you will believe every word you say, and even act on it. For example, you feel as if a casual comment to a stranger like 'If you can't give up smoking, you may as well go and jump in front of a train' will be followed by a news bulletin the next day saying that, due to an unexpected accident on the line, the Intercity 125 will now be delayed while the tracks are cleared.

Seriously, though, there is comfort and satisfaction in knowing that you are now starting a career in which you will try to spend the rest of your working life being paid a decent salary to do good things to people. When as a doctor you finally retire and reflect on your life's achievements, you will not be counting the number of rich so and sos you've managed to make even richer on the Stock Exchange via shrewd wheelings and dealings. No, instead, you'll be noting the number of people who have been hugely grateful to you for your care, kindness and attention, support and help.

Another bonus with medicine is that, from the day you start as a house officer, you can be sure that, should you so wish it, you can be fully employed for the rest of your life. Friends doing managerial courses with high-powered companies in the City can be hired and fired depending on the state of the economy without so much as a 'thank you'. Doctors in England are in demand – there is a shortage – and, apart from that, the government isn't about to spend £200,000 on training you up so you can be on the dole. There are even attempts nowadays for certain Trust hospitals to head-hunt top consultants and try to lure them to new jobs with lucrative offers and financial incentives. Who would have dreamt of it 20 years ago?

Happy to be a doctor?

- Decent income.
- Job security for life.
- Respected by society.
- Spend your life doing good to people.

The structure of the house year

The house year is when you start to live the lifestyle of a doctor – a lifestyle that will be the same for the next five years of your life and only change when you graduate to being a GP or consultant.

The house year is actually composed of two six-month jobs. Currently, these are one six-month attachment to a medical ward and one six-month attachment to a surgical ward. There are always reviews and changes to the medical career structure, and the house year is subject to these, too. Indeed, recently, in a few areas, six months in general practice has been introduced in place of one of the above attachments. This will either be increasingly phased in nationwide or it will fail to succeed and be consigned to the dustbin – we will wait and see which it is to be. Despite such adjustments, the basic structure is well established and so will remain, for the foreseeable future, a combination of six-month jobs, in rotation.

The positive aspects

The bonus of this structure is that, as a junior doctor, in a relatively short space of time, you can experience numerous different jobs. For example, in the five years since I qualified in 1993, I've done a medical and surgical job as a house officer, and have since worked in accident and emergency, obstetrics and gynaecology and psychiatry departments and had a further medical job, all as a senior house officer (the next rank up).

The negative aspects

The disadvantage of the system is the fact that you can't really settle during this time. Every six months you start a new job, and every six months you have to get to know a whole new set of skills, specialist knowledge, ward procedures, consultants and even hospitals. Inevitably, to start with you feel somewhat helpless and useless until you've found your feet, and it may take a few months before you actually start to feel confident about what you are doing. That then only leaves a few months of 'happy' work before you change jobs and feel useless again!

Another disadvantage is the fact that many doctors will actually do these jobs in different hospitals, often in totally different parts of the country. The current practice in the UK is for all jobs to start and end on the first Wednesday of the months of February and August. Why Wednesday? Well, apparently, the middle of the week is the most sensible and convenient time to switch jobs as it causes the least inconvenience to the hospital's managers. Unfortunately, if you are finishing one job in London and starting your next in Liverpool, say, it means you're going to have one hell of a night transferring all of your stuff so that, come Wednesday morning, you are all set and ready in your new hospital. Logic would suggest that a weekend changeover would be more appropriate for doctors. However, this would mean that hospitals would have to employ cleaners at the weekends to tidy rooms between the outgoing and incoming doctors, and provide a manager to organize all the paperwork and keys. All this involves extra hospital spending, so doctors just have to lump it.

What will I actually be doing?

When working in a hospital as a pre-registration house officer, you will be attached to a 'firm' of doctors, led normally by one specific consultant who, in effect, is your boss. You will work on that consultant's ward, see their patients and present these patients to them on ward rounds (that is, you tell the consultant about the day-to-day progress of the ward patients).

You will be expected by your consultant to be reasonably familiar and up to date on all of these patients, to keep the patients' notes current and record new information well, and organize any tests or investigations that they deem to be appropriate. You will be assisted and guided in this process by your immediately senior colleagues in your team – namely, the senior house officer (SHO) and registrar (more on these roles later). Together, you work as a team to make sure all that needs to be done is done, and that any problems are recognized at an early stage and acted on.

As well as the team of doctors, you will also be guided and advised by nursing staff, physiotherapists, occupational therapists, speech and language therapists, specialist nurses and so on, who are all players in the big hospital network of staff. They all work together and use each other's particular skills to get the patients better.

By the end of the year as a house officer, you may well feel like a glorified secretary, with all the paperwork and job-running. However, in fact, you will have learnt more skills and acquired more abilities than you ever did as a medical student, even if you don't realize it at the time.

The on call commitment

Working hours are pretty well set now as a standard 9 to 5 day, or with an 8 am start in most surgical jobs. Additional hours are required to cover the hospital overnight – the so-called 'on call' commitment. Being on call means working a normal 9 to 5 day and then just keeping going all the way through the night until the next morning, when you will probably work the 9 to 5 bit again before going home and collapsing in an exhausted heap. Weekends can be even more fun, when you start work Saturday morning and finish Monday afternoon, so that you finally get home after a 56-hour shift. Nice!

When you apply for jobs as a house officer, you are of course entitled and expected to know just what the on call commitment is for the job. It may be a 'one in five', which is when you work overnight every fifth night and every fifth weekend. It may be a 'one in four', sometimes even a 'one in three'. Obviously, the more frequently you're on call, the more knackering the job will be.

Current nationally agreed guidelines suggest that no junior doctor in a hard-pressed post should be required to be on duty for more than 72 hours a week if working on an on call rota. In practice, it often happens that you do work more hours than this, and there's rarely anyone to complain to about it. A standard consultants' response to juniors bemoaning their lot would be them reminding juniors that, in their day, they all used to work a one in two. The ultimate aim, as I understand it, is to get all junior doctors working a maximum of 56 hours a week, but that target remains a fair way off.

Summary

- Six-monthly jobs mean lots of moving.
- House officers can feel undervalued, even abused.
- The on call commitment plays havoc with your social life.
- You realize that, even after five years, you still don't know much.
- However, if, after a year of being a house officer, you have kept your consultants happy and managed not to kill anyone through stupidity, you will have completed your pre-registration year and will be formally registered as a qualified doctor by the General Medical Council (GMC). You've made it!

4

What happens in the senior house officer years?

Doctors quite rightly feel like they have finally started to make it on the career ladder when they 'graduate' from the pre-registration house year to become fully registered qualified doctors, with the consequent promotion to the heady rank of senior house officer (SHO).

Choosing specialties

On reflection, it is normally during the clinical years at medical school when students first start to have an idea about which specialist areas of medicine are of interest to them. I and some of my friends, however, still had no idea what we wanted to do, but realized what we *didn't* want to be. In my own case, I knew by my third year at medical school that I definitely did not want to be a surgeon. In this way a gradual process of elimination or selection occurs.

At medical school, we are all allowed to dream about what we may or may not want to be. During the house year, the need for a more formal decision starts to become necessary. In that year, the options as to what specialties are available are pretty much limited to medicine and surgery, but in the SHO years, the whole hospital opens its doors to you and so the options are almost endless. Hence the need for an SHO to have some idea of what it is they want to learn more about so they can apply for the appropriate jobs.

In practice, most SHOs choose one of three options, which are really quite different from each other. For this reason, I shall deal with each one separately.

- **SHO specialist hospital rotations.** These are normally composed of four six-month jobs, so totalling two years' work. They aim to take an SHO through the necessary basic training in a single specialty up to the level of knowledge required to be promoted to the next level – a hospital registrar.
- **SHO vocational training schemes.** These are normally composed of up to four six-month hospital posts in a variety of specialties. The posts provide doctors with an increased breadth of knowledge in a variety of areas of medicine, which act as the foundations for becoming a GP.
- **'The independents'.** These are the many SHOs who, for a variety of reasons, do not want to commit to either of the above, but would rather apply for six-monthly jobs as and when they wish to. They may at any stage choose to opt into either of the above schemes or, as a result of their planning, reach equivalent experience via their own individual selections.

The SHO specialist hospital rotations

There are at least 20 hospital specializations from which budding consultants can choose. These include the most obvious – obstetrics and gynaecology, psychiatry, ophthalmology, orthopaedics, dermatology, paediatrics, medicine (which itself is composed of specialties in their own right – respiratory, gastroenterology, cardiology, haematology, endocrinology and so on) and surgery (which, again, has its own specialties – vascular, cardiac, gastroenterology, breast, transplants and so on). The first step towards establishing the required knowledge in any of these specialties is to spend two years as an SHO gaining the necessary experience and further examination qualifications.

Getting on to a specialist scheme

Schemes are advertised on a weekly basis in the *British Medical Journal (BMJ)* – standard reading material for junior doctors. You apply for them just like any other job – by sending in a CV with a covering letter and, if possible, actually visiting the hospital and meeting the consultants with whom you would be working prior to the actual interviews.

Successful applicants will be assured of two years' worth of work with formal teaching sessions and exposure to their chosen specialties. A two-year medical rotation, for example, may be composed of six months each in cardiology, respiratory, haematology and care of the elderly. An equivalent surgical rotation may consist of work in the specialties of vascular, urology, gastroenterology and accident and emergency.

The exams

All specialties have their own specific examinations that the SHOs are expected to pass during this two-year period. These are the proverbial nightmare examinations – written papers, multiple-choice papers, 'live' exams (vivas) – all with extremely low pass rates, meaning that some people take up to six attempts before they finally pass. Failure to get over this hurdle effectively prevents a doctor from pursuing that particular specialty.

These exams are the college exams, and passing them allows a doctor to become a 'member' of that particular college. For example, a medical SHO would need to sit the Member of the Royal College of Physicians (MRCP) exam, while a surgeon would try to pass the Fellow of the Royal College of Surgeons (FRCS) exam.

Not only are these exams very hard to pass – comparisons have been made with the 'eye of a needle' passage in the Bible – but they are also extremely expensive, costing up to £400 per attempt, which is not refunded if you fail them. Hence, failing more than once can spell the loss of a summer holiday.

These exams are not just hard in terms of their content but because revision for them has to be packed in at home in your personal time after working the long hospital hours that are expected. This is one of the aspects of a trainee doctor's life that is not often taken into account. It is not just about working the 70 hours per week in hospital, but the other 20 hours of revision done during the nights that is required to pass these ridiculously hard exams. If you are at school at the moment and think that once you've done your 'A' levels you'll almost be at the end of your examination days, then you'd better think again. In ten years' time, after you've already done five years at medical school and a year as a house officer, you'll still be revising well into the early hours of the morning to pass these ones.

The hospitals do see it as being in their best interests to help you pass. No SHO in their right mind is going to sign up to a two-year scheme with a hospital that has a zero pass rate. Indeed, if any hospital does continually fail to provide adequate teaching and support for its SHOs, it can have its official status as a training scheme revoked by the powers that be. As a result, all hospitals will grant periods of study leave to their doctors (up to 30 days per year) and will also attempt to come up with the funds required to send them on specialized revision courses to help them pass. The cost of the exam itself however comes straight out of the doctors' own pockets.

As a result, the aims of most SHOs on two-year training schemes are to gain as much clinical experience as they can on the ward and in outpatient clinics, while also working and revising to pass the appropriate exams. If, after two years, all the jobs have been completed satisfactorily and the exams have been passed, then the SHO is able to apply for the next ladder up – the registrar jobs. There are always exceptions to prove the rule, and certainly there are some registrars who will have reached that level *before* passing the exams, but, in reality, they are really only delaying the inevitable.

SHO vocational training schemes

Any doctor who has decided that they would rather be a GP or family doctor than a hospital consultant, still needs to gain a greater knowledge than medical school alone is able to provide, in a variety of specialties, so that they may use that knowledge in their community work. Hence, vocational training schemes offer a variety of jobs over, normally, a two-year period to provide for this need. To this end, the two years may consist of a combination of psychiatry, obstetrics, gynaecology, general medicine, care of the elderly, paediatrics, ear, nose and throat, accident and emergency, and so on. These jobs may last anywhere between three and six months each, and some schemes will include jobs that other schemes do not. Thus a budding GP can scan the *British Medical Journal* for a scheme that they feel will be of most use to them.

Diplomas

Almost all of these jobs run side by side with the jobs the hospital specialist SHOs are doing, and can be equally demanding. Likewise, although the GP trainees do not need to sit the college exams talked about above, they will still be expected to do some book work and often sit exams that are more relevant to the ultimate goal of being a GP. These include diploma exams in specialties such as obstetrics and gynaecology (the DRCOG) or care of the elderly (Dip. Care of Elderly) and other courses, such as those on family planning and child health surveillance, while perhaps also doing training in procedures carried out on a regular basis in general practice, such as minor surgery or fitting contraceptives.

Again, the hospitals endeavour to provide the time and funding for study leave for these exams and courses. Something slightly different, though, is that often these two years, which are based in hospital, provide knowledge and skills that may not initially seem to be relevant to general practice. Thus, many vocational training schemes try to ensure that their GP trainees are released from their hospital commitments for half a day per week so that they can focus on their ultimate goal of becoming a GP and try to maintain and develop other skills that might otherwise fade away while working in a hospital setting. This is time that is highly valued by most GP trainees, but, unfortunately, due to the massive pressures of hospital jobs, often it has to be forgone because of hospital demands.

VTR forms

After each six months spent as an SHO in a hospital job, the GP trainee gets a form called a VTR form signed by the relevant consultant. The requirements at the time of writing are for GP trainees to obtain at least four of these forms as proof to the Royal College of General Practitioners that enough general experience has been obtained for that trainee to work as a registrar in general practice – again the next step up on the ladder.

The independents

All doctors, no matter whether they wish to be consultants or GPs, are currently expected to be SHOs for at least two years. There are plans afoot to alter this slightly in respect of GPs, but the situation remains as stated above for now.

The advantages

As we have seen, many junior doctors finish their house year with no specific ideas as to what they ultimately wish to be. This means it would be inappropriate for them to try to apply for a specialized training scheme like those described above, but this is not as big a problem as it may sound. The standard six-month job structure means that doctors can try lots of different specialties without the fear of making a long-term commitment to something that they may find they do not enjoy.

Going independent allows you to experiment in all sorts of different fields of medicine until one is finally found that proves attractive. It also allows you to choose, should you desire to, to take a break from work for a while without having a commitment to a two-year scheme This time is often used to go travelling or to try working in other countries, most commonly Australia and New Zealand. All this experience does add up to produce a doctor with a wide set of experiences and knowledge, and if the four VTR forms are obtained along the way, then these jobs in themselves can be a substitute for the more formal schemes described above.

The disadvantages

Going independent does have some disadvantages. The teaching and study leave options are sometimes not freely available, and for every six-month job you want to do, new CVs have to be sent, interviews conducted and so on. As a result, in return for the freedom, there is a sense of insecurity, as you never know exactly where you may be in six months' time. Most doctors who are only on six-month contacts resign themselves to living in hospital accommodation, as landlords tend to be reluctant to rent properties on such a short-term basis. Also, joining local sports clubs, getting into local sports teams or getting involved in local communities all becomes less realistic when you're only going to be there for six months. That's why so many people finally get signed on to a formal two-year scheme.

Ultimately, the SHO years are not the be-all and end-all, but merely a stepping-stone to greater things. Thus, although there is no limit on how many SHO jobs you can do or how long you stay at that grade, the incentives of the better pay and more friendly lifestyle that come with the higher grades tend to persuade SHOs to focus quickly on something that they want to specialize in.

What does an SHO actually do?

The work of a house officer consists of trailing more senior doctors on ward rounds, filling out forms, pushing the ward trolley, carrying the notes and trying to remember a hundred different jobs your consultant expects to be done by the following day. To many house officers, it seems a bit like serving time before being 'released' into the real work of doctoring.

When you first become an SHO, however, the work becomes a bit more interesting. You are now a fully registered, qualified doctor and probably working within a scheme with the aim of becoming something specific, like a surgeon, physician or GP. Hence, your aims are more focused, your ambitions clearer, your targets set.

The book work is still as tedious as ever, but at least you can now learn something one night and then apply it on a ward round the next day. You can even teach it to your house officer, if you are fortunate enough to have one (in the present scheme of things, you will only have one if you are doing a medical or surgical job).

As well as ward work, many SHOs are expected to see patients in the outpatient clinics, although, more often than not, advice has to be sought on a regular basis from the more senior doctors as to what exactly to do with these patients. Still, it is a change of scenery from the ward work, and at least gives you the chance to sit down at times!

The hours are still long, with the on call commitment as great as ever. Many SHOs actually find their nights on call more stressful than when they were just house officers – the greater responsibilities are a heavy burden to carry. Still, on the whole, at least you actually feel as though you are applying your skills and knowledge as a doctor directly to your patients, while learning new skills along the way. It is a busy and stressful time, but it is also productive and exciting.

There is often a subtle change in the consultants' attitude towards you as well. No longer are you the irritating and useless medical student, nor any longer the 'doctor in nappies' house officer. You are now quite a valuable member of the team, one whose factual knowledge may actually be more up to date than that of the consultants themselves. You are also the one person who can make the subtle difference between a ward round that goes quickly and efficiently or slowly and tediously.

Study leave is also a new much valued and important opportunity for the SHOs. It is special because it means that you are off the ward, not seeing patients but spending your time doing something that is to your own personal benefit. This could be spent staying at home, doing book work for the exams or on a course learning about new skills and concepts. Either way, you are out of hospital, doing something of benefit to you alone, and you get paid as if you were in hospital anyway! Great!

Other aspects of life as an SHO

Apart from the medical aspect, these SHO years are all about other things as well. For example, this will probably be the first time since leaving school that your bank balance starts to look healthy. As a result, many SHOs whizz off on skiing trips in the winter and take up windsurfing, scuba-diving or other equally ambitious sports in the summer. I have one friend who restarted ballet classes, another who resumed Tae Kwondo lessons. An amazing number of new cars appear outside an SHO's house when a party is held and, even more scarily, an amazing number of these cars will have baby seats strapped inside. Yes, indeed, the SHO years are the first years when doctors really start to tie knots and make commitments.

The advantages of being in the medical profession start to become evident at this point, such as when you want to secure a mortgage. The fact that, barring disaster, you are almost guaranteed employment for the rest of your working life means that, although many SHOs are still trying to pay off student debts, they can secure substantial mortgages from the banks. With mortgages come weddings, and the once outrageous doctors' mess parties give way to more civilized dinners with carefully selected wines. Weekends away may be spent romancing in isolated rented cottages or log-burning farmhouse bed and breakfasts. The basic rule is that the harder you work, the more you should enjoy your playtime.

Two-year commitments to schemes allow doctors to rent or buy properties, finally escaping from the uninspiring greyness of hospital accommodation. Hobbies that have been difficult to keep going while living in hospital accommodation are able to resurface. It's not easy to cook decent meals on a Baby Belling, especially when anything remotely tasty left in communal fridges tends to disappear, but once you are in your own home with a four hob twin oven, well, the possibilities are endless! You will also be able to join local clubs, sports teams, golf clubs even, and actually venture out of the confines of the hospital.

Unfortunately, this is also a crunch time for a lot of relationships. Many become established while at university and struggle through the house year before being starved to death in the SHO years. Time is scarce and precious as an SHO, with long working hours and exam revision requirements meaning that genuine free time is often scarce and then you are lacking in energy.

This is why doctors often go out with and marry other doctors. We understand each other's commitment to our jobs and the way we often feel after a stressful day at work. When trying to unwind from a bad day by telling your partner about it, it helps if that partner has a medical training and understands the decisions, stresses and implications that are worrying you. Fellow doctors accept the indignity and grimness of having free weekends cancelled at short notice because of contractual commitments. Fellow doctors accept that even on holiday they are still on duty, for example if someone should suddenly fall ill or have an accident.

Generally speaking, doctors tend to be supportive and caring people, spending their days giving themselves to their patients, and so, often, at the end of the day they just want a little bit of sympathy to be shown to them. It takes a very special partner to put up with all of this, and many people who are not involved in the medical profession decide that this is not a lifestyle they wish to marry into.

Summary

- Two to three years are spent starting to specialize in an area of medicine.
- There are three basic options – hospital schemes, vocational training or going 'independent'.
- Work becomes more interesting and challenging – ward work is intermixed with outpatient clinics, theatre time and paperwork.
- Revision for huge exams has to be stuffed into the small spaces between the long hours worked.
- As knowledge increases, so does respect from senior colleagues.
- Having a better salary and a secure job allows for holidays, homes, cars and fun.
- Relationships that have lasted this far are made or broken now as the work commitment dominates life.
- SHOs end up knowing really quite a lot, and feel good and useful at work. In case you hadn't realized it already, it should now be clear that life as a doctor is not just a 9 to 5 job; it is a career and a lifestyle that will dominate your life, no matter how hard you try not to allow it to. This is what being a doctor is all about.

5

What are the registrar years like?

All doctors working up through the ranks to become either consultants or GPs will have worked side by side as SHOs, as stated in the previous chapter, even though their individual goals are different. Once the relevant experience and exams have been gained as an SHO, the next rank to be promoted to is that of registrar. It is finally at this point where the training separates those wanting to work in hospitals from those wanting to be GPs

The GP registrar

Just to recap, a doctor wishing to become a GP will, by this stage, have spent five years at medical school, one year as a house officer, two years as an SHO, possibly as part of a specific vocational training scheme (VTS). Some examinations will have been sat already, including, of course, finals, but also probably various diplomas in subjects such as paediatrics, obstetrics and gynaecology or care of the elderly. Other relevant courses are often completed during those SHO years, including resuscitation skills, minor surgery training and child health surveillance.

What's so different?

Almost the whole of a doctor's experience and training so far has been based in hospital, but now, as a registrar, if you are wanting to be a GP, you start to learn about it in the only appropriate setting for this – a GP's surgery. There are numerous advertisements in the *BMJ* every week for surgeries seeking GP registrars, so finding a place as a registrar is not difficult. Once a practice is chosen, you will work under the guidance of a qualified GP within that practice during the year.

The working environment

Your working life is suddenly very different. Hospital outpatient clinics are replaced with morning and afternoon clinics, ward rounds are replaced with home visits, and the noises of the wards and your bleeper are replaced by the new working environment of your own consulting room and phone. The traditional hospital 'firm' of house officer, SHO, registrar and consultant, is replaced in general practice with a much broader and larger 'team'. This will include not only all the GPs within a practice, but also a practice manager, front desk receptionists and secretaries, practice nurses, district nurses, social workers – the list goes on. As a GP registrar you have to learn to become a team player, recognizing and using all the other team members' skills and abilities to the total benefit of your patients.

The patients

The patients themselves are different as well in almost every sense. Their problems will be different and unfamiliar to a doctor who has so far trained only in the illnesses that bring people to hospital. The treatments required for illnesses seen in GPs' surgeries will be based not solely on a diagnosis of what they are, but be guided by each patient's unique requirements and circumstances. Patients' attitudes towards their health are different, too, and their individuality will become more evident to a GP than can ever be apparent when working in a hospital setting.

How can I explain this better? Well, if you have ever entered a hospital and walked through the wards looking for a friend or relative, you may have noticed that it can be quite hard to recognize the person you're looking for. Hospitals have this strange effect of depersonalizing people, making all patients look remarkably the same. All the wards invariably look the same, they almost always have the same antiseptic smell, the beds are the same, the chairs are the same, the patients are mostly wearing hospital pyjamas or gowns, which make them look the same – everyone just blends into the overall working environment the hospital creates. The patients, as a final indignity, are invariably reduced to bed numbers ('Bed 3 is being sick, Bed 5 needs a commode, and the man in Bed 9 looks like he's about to die . . . '). Because the occupants of these beds are sick, they often don't even realize it's happened to them. Their attitude towards their health is different as well. All patients arriving in hospital are already aware of the likelihood that they have a serious illness (otherwise they wouldn't be going there). They are therefore prepared in their minds for a full physical examination, blood tests, X-rays and anything else the hospital doctors feel is necessary.

General practice, however, is different. The patients invariably walk into the practice fully clothed, wearing their own clothes, feeling and acting like the individuals they are. Alternatively, they may require a home visit, where it's not the patient who feels as if they are in an alien environment, but the doctor. It is, after all, a privilege to be invited into anyone's home. Thus, the patients' attitudes are different. In general practice, the patients arrive for their ten-minute appointment, seeking reassurance about what they perceive to be a mild ailment. If the GP discovers that, in fact, the ailment is more serious, in that ten-minute session the GP will need to persuade that patient to undress, dress, have extra tests done, possibly go into hospital, and maybe even break some bad news. Now the patient wasn't expecting this, doesn't want it and will probably go into denial. They can be quite formidable opponents!

Hospital patient	Typical GP's patient
Normally, are ill	Normally, are in relatively good health
Understand they are ill	Expect themselves to be well or well soon
Are prepared for examinations	Are fully dressed and wish to stay so
Are prepared for investigations	Are suspicious of investigations
Expect to stay for several days	Expect to be going home in ten minutes
Feel insecure in the alien environment	Feel safe in their own environment
Do mostly what the doctors tell them to do while in hospital	Do mostly whatever they feel like doing once they've walked out of the door
Take tablets as requested, at the right time, when given to them by the nurses	Take tablets for as long as they feel like it, when they remember
Will probably never see that doctor again once out of hospital	Will have to get on with the GP for many years to come

What are the challenges for a GP registrar?

A GP registrar needs to change their attitude towards the patients so it is appropriate to the environment and expectations of staff and patients, new skills need to be acquired quickly and new knowledge gained. Consulting skills need to be refined so that important material can be sifted from the immaterial quickly in a consultation, and new listening skills developed to help you recognize when the presenting complaint of a runny nose is an excuse for coming to see the doctor about something much more serious. A broader knowledge of a patient's circumstances is required than is the case in hospitals as a sprained ankle may be merely an inconvenience to a young athlete, but a disaster to an elderly lady living at home alone, with no home help and an upstairs toilet and bedroom. GP registrars therefore have to start thinking of their patients in a truly 'holistic' manner. This means thinking about their long-term wellbeing as well as short-term illness, taking into account their style of life, accommodation, general physical and mental health, availability of family and friends for help, financial support, as well as patients' expectations, hopes and beliefs.

How long does it last?

The GP registrars' training period lasts for only one year. This is in stark contrast to the hospital registrar scheme, which lasts much longer (see page 39). This is great for someone who is tired of doing all sorts of different jobs and wants to just settle down in their chosen career of GP. There is, however, an awful lot to pack into this one year.

The implications of the differences between patients in hospitals and patients in GPs' surgeries are that GP registrars have to reappraise the whole dynamics of patient care, learn about new illnesses and new problems and develop lots of new skills. Also, you have to get to grips with the workings of a typical general practice. Fundholding has introduced the need to have some financial management skills as such practices are now medium-sized businesses. Each GP within the practice will, for example, be responsible for maintaining the health of up to 2000 patients in their care. Budgets need to be managed, especially in relation to the costs of prescriptions, and regular research and audit work is conducted to make sure that the money is being spent as wisely as possible. Money is always tight, so it is up to the doctors within a practice to provide the best patient care they can for their patients within the financial constraints imposed on them by the government of the day.

One year goes very quickly when there's so much to do, and at the end of it many registrars feel they are still only just getting to grips with the fundamentals of the job. With so much to accomplish, it is likely that this period of training will be increased to at least 18 months, if not longer.

What are the ideal qualifications to gain by the end of the year?

The absolute minimum required for a doctor to practice as a GP is to gain a pass in a series of exams that are currently called 'summative assessment'. The assessment is the GP's equivalent of a car's MOT – the absolute minimum required to be considered safe to practice.

Summative assessment consists of a multiple-choice exam paper, a project based on experience gained in general practice (an audit), a set of videotaped actual consultations with patients (taped, of course, after the patient has given written consent to this), and a final written report from your GP trainer stating that you are safe to work.

In practice, most registrars try to pass the equivalent of the big exams that the hospital SHOs sit – the membership exam or, in this particular case, the Member of the Royal College of General Practitioners (MRCGP) Exam. This, like summative assessment, has several parts, including written papers, multiple-choice papers, videos and a viva (a live exam). It costs about £500 to sit the exam, each time you need to sit it. It is, however the gold standard for budding GPs and will be expected by all good practices looking for a new partner.

A final list of qualifications and completed courses for a fully trained GP could typically include:

- Bachelor of Medicine
- summative assessment
- Member of the Royal College of General Practitioners (MRCGP)

- Diploma of the Royal College of Obstetricians and Gynaecologists (DRCOG)
- Child Health Surveillance
- Minor Surgery
- Family Planning
- Advanced Life Support (ALS)
- Diploma of Child Health (DCH)/Care of the Elderly.

Not surprisingly, most GP registrars feel they have done their fair share of exams by the time they qualify to the level that makes them eligible to be a GP and, not surprisingly, wonder just what exactly they have spent the last five years of their lives doing apart from working to accumulate extra letters after their names!

Where does this all lead to?

Although it is possible to become a fully qualified GP as young as 30 years old (as opposed to consultants who rarely qualify much before the age of 35), most qualified registrars feel unwilling to commit themselves to a practice and become a member of a partnership immediately – that is, become a GP 'principal'. The majority of newly qualified GPs take the opportunity after their training year, once all the exams are over, to go on an extended trip abroad. They often use their qualifications to enable them to work while they are away and, thus, gain new experiences and have a holiday all at the same time.

Those who do apply for jobs within a practice straight away and succeed in becoming principals face the start of a long career as a GP, with all that that entails. The shorter training period required to become a GP compared with that required to become a consultant has obvious attractions for those who are fed up with being a junior doctor, but it also has its disadvantages. The main one is that a 30-year-old in general practice will be carrying a lot more responsibility and weight on their shoulders than a hospital doctor of the same age. The main difference, though, between a hospital registrar and a GP registrar lies in what the individual doctor's hopes and aspirations are, and what kind of lifestyle they want. Not everyone wishes to be a GP, nor even has the ability to be one, and the same applies to consultancy. It is a genuine case of 'each to their own'. There is no difference in terms of the total levels of skill or importance each role has. Indeed, hospital and community doctors have to have a symbiotic relationship, relying on each other, neither being able to be effective without the other's help.

What does hospital registrar training involve?

If you are a junior doctor who is specializing and wish to become a consultant, then you will have to become a hospital registrar first. To reach this position, you must first have already completed five years at medical school, one year as a house officer and at least two years as an SHO working in relevant subjects, while also obtaining the relevant membership exams.

The hospital registrar training scheme is now a standard five-year programme following the recommendations made by a man called Calman a few years ago, and is considerably shorter than registrar training used to be. Calman effectively streamlined the training and thereby reduced the time taken for a registrar to become a consultant.

Most of the current junior doctors see this as a good thing as it means they get to where they want to be sooner than used to be the case. However, some of the older consultants see this rapid training process as potentially dangerous. In their view, the many years that used to be spent as a junior were vital for building up the necessary broad experience that they themselves have obtained, and they fear that the newer 'Calman'-trained consultants will lack necessary skills and expertise due to their briefer training. Only time will tell on that one, but, as a whole, the five-year training means that anyone staying in hospital life can see an end point to their time as a junior and, hence, it makes the whole lifestyle more attractive than it was previously.

The old system used to mean that a junior would first spend many years as a registrar before being promoted to senior registrar (SR). This effectively meant that any firm of doctors would have a fairly experienced doctor being covered by an even more experienced doctor. As a result, it used to be very rare for a consultant to be called out in the middle of the night to help with a problem – the SR would almost always be able to handle any overnight emergency. Now that the SR buffer has been removed, it is possible that a first-year registrar (who is still really rather inexperienced) will be trying to cope with overnight emergencies and will realize that they, in fact, do not have the necessary skills yet. Their only option – as there is no SR – is to call out a consultant. Hence, although consultants are getting younger, they are also getting called out more than they used to be.

How do I get on a training scheme?

To get on a five-year registrar training scheme involves updating your CV and ensuring that references from previous consultants you've worked for are up to scratch. Without good references, the chances of being shortlisted for an interview are minimal.

Just what you have to do to obtain a good reference from a consultant you've worked for as an SHO is subject to conjecture. What many older consultants would perceive as being a good reference would include phrases such as 'happy to work long hours' or 'always willing to fill in at short notice' or, perhaps, 'puts on a brave face, never one to complain'. This is always in the back of an SHOs mind during the SHO years and explains why you will very rarely see an SHO argue, disagree or complain. If you stand your ground and refuse to be pushed around as an SHO, the chances are that you'll never get the references you need to climb the ladder.

Not only do SHOs need to ensure that their references and CVs are likely to hit the spot, but many of the consultants will expect to have met budding applicants prior to the formal interviews for an 'informal' chat. This leads to most junior doctors spending days off work, travelling potentially hundreds of miles to meet the necessary consultants prior to the interview itself. These informal interviews are a hazardous affair, commonly referred to as brown-nosing, and often don't go quite according to plan.

I have several friends who travelled a long way for these informal meetings only to find that when they see the relevant consultant's secretary, the consultant is stuck in theatre, delayed in outpatients or has lost a ball on the eighteenth hole and isn't in a good mood! When the meetings do go ahead, they can be anything from a passing handshake in the corridor, a cup of coffee and a quick chat, to an invitation to spend the rest of the afternoon assisting them in theatre. After all that, the consultant may decide that they don't like you, in which case all you've achieved is a wasted day off work and extra mileage on the car!

Once the appropriate amount of brown-nosing has occurred, you may be lucky enough to get on the short list for an official interview. At the interview itself, you need to be brimming with life, prepared for questions on anything from the philosophical to the latest research on rare diseases, and generally shine out from the other applicants. If luck is on your side, then you may just land the job!

The basics of registrar training

- Five-year Calman training programme.
- End result – you are an accredited registrar ready for consultancy.

The interview system requires:

- membership exams
- good references
- brown-nosing
- a bit of luck.

What about the job itself?

The step from SHO to registrar is not to be underestimated as the nature of the work starts to change quite fundamentally.

A shift in emphasis

As an SHO, virtually all work time was spent doing routine patient examinations, taking blood tests, doing discharge summaries, signing prescription charts and going on daily ward rounds, during which you would rarely have to make any vitally important decisions. In effect, you were exactly what your title suggested – a senior house officer. As a registrar, however, you can, in theory, leave most of these mundane tasks behind. Outpatient clinics, specialist clinics, research work, operating lists, presentations, teaching sessions – all start to take over your previous work. Registrars are expected to write papers for medical journals, present research findings at conferences around the country or sometimes even abroad, act as representative of their consultant in their absence and even challenge the consultant with new thoughts and ideas learnt during training. The aim, after all, is to leave you with all the skills required by the end of the five years to be a consultant.

How ward rounds change

Ward rounds become slightly more challenging, too. When you were a house officer or SHO, all the difficult decisions could be left until the registrar or consultant was available to guide and advise. Now, all of a sudden, you are that registrar and all those difficult decisions are now down to you! What's more, when your consultant is off on holiday or sick, the chances are that it'll be left to you to hold things together until they get back. You will start to feel the real weight of the responsibilities that come with being a consultant.

Becoming a specialist

The five years of the training are spent gaining the specialist skills and knowledge required for your chosen field in medicine. In effect, you are lifted from the grade of competent but barely specialized SHO to the level of a consultant. During this time, your knowledge becomes more highly focused on the one area of medicine you have picked to specialize in. A casual flick through the *BMJ*'s advertisements section reveals the training schemes on offer – and they are all highly specialized. For example, five years doing geriatric medicine, six years doing orthopaedic surgery, five years doing paediatrics with paediatric cardiology, five years urologist training.

The on call commitment

On top of all this, the registrars are still expected to provide ward cover and work similar hours to those of an SHO, including the ongoing requirement to provide overnight on call cover. In some specialties, you may in fact find your overnight workload is as heavy or even heavier than is the case for the juniors working with you. This is especially true in the surgical fields of medicine, where anything other than a simple appendectomy would probably require a registrar's presence. In some fields of medicine, the night workload is particularly heavy. For example, in accident and emergency, the SHOs work a shift system during the day up until midnight and then never actually work overnight – this is left to the specialist registrars to do as it is often felt that the work here is too intense, stressful and important for an SHO to be left alone to look after overnight.

Study time

Meanwhile, although as a registrar you may not have any examinations to sit (these were all done as an SHO) the evening work commitments continue (although they are perhaps at a less intense level). You will need to prepare teaching sessions, read journals, specialist books and so on.

Other aspects of life as a registrar

It is unlikely that you will be based in just one hospital throughout the five years of registrar training. Most schemes will require maybe one year in one city, then another year somewhere else and so on, generally all within one particular region, until the five-year period is up. This, in effect, makes it very difficult for a registrar to be able to commit to living in any one area, and the need to pack up your bags and move to new rented accommodation with each job becomes monotonously familiar. Many registrars are, by this stage in their lives, either married or trying to establish the foundations of a stable relationship, so this continual moving process can be a pain .

Still, at least there is the security of knowing that you have a five-year working contract, the money will continue to flow in and that, at the end of the five years, you should be ready for a permanent consultant post at a hospital.

Does anything else need to be done before the training is over?

Many doctors find that they develop an interest in research work and apply for an extra period after the five years is up as a research fellow. This post requires less ward and outpatient responsibility and, often, a minimal on call commitment, allowing you to spend time at the forefront of medical discoveries. This often looks great on a CV and allows you to gain experience in setting up and running research work that might well be possible in the coming years as a consultant. A fellowship often lasts for one or two years on top of the five years of the Calman scheme.

What happens after the training is over?

Once the scheme has been completed satisfactorily, you can apply for accreditation, and once you have received your accreditation certificate you can apply for consultant jobs. You should try to do this within a year. One of the most frustrating and positively irritating aspects of the medical set-up is the fact that after spending five years working your butt off to gain accreditation, you have to pay £400 for the certificate itself!

6

What is it like being a GP?

General practice is the place where, statistically, almost half of all medical graduates end up. It is an honourable and highly skilled profession that extends incredibly high standards of service and care to the general population, while always trying to cope with the mainly politically driven changes that force frequent and stressful transformations on it. Almost like a snake that sheds its skin, general practice has to shed old ways and adopt new ones with every change of government. Just as fundholding was established under the Conservatives, so a new set of guidelines inspired by a Labour government have now been released as part of a White Paper that will yet again throw the organization of general practice into confusion. For better or worse, things are destined to change.

'I remember when...'

A while ago, a rather senior (in age and standing) GP recounted to me what it had been like when he first qualified as a GP. In those days, there was no specific training for general practice, and he recalled that joining the Royal College of General Practitioners was rather like joining an old boys' club. Based in a rural area, his day consisted of arriving at his practice, a single-handed affair, at around 9 am, by which time a queue of motley looking locals would have gathered for his attention. During the course of the morning, he would gradually see them, one by one, and catch up on their lives, well-being and health, until the queue had been accounted for. After this, there might have been a small number of visits to do, some of which would have been of a medical nature (but a patient would only dare call a doctor for a home visit *in extremis*) or a social nature (the monthly visit 'expected' by the more affluent locals).

After the visits, came a round of golf. Now, this doctor's house backed on to the ninth hole, so, in the event of any emergencies, he could always be contacted as he passed on to the tenth tee. An afternoon at the practice would then see an end to the day. One of the local population might have summoned him in the middle of the night, but only if it was truly urgent.

The modern practice

Times change, and that GP has had to adapt over the years as the profession has become far less easy-going. In a typical practice, all patients are now seen by appointment and, due to the large number of patients each GP has to care for, those appointments are limited to ten minutes each. Single-handed practices are being replaced with super-centres, with five, ten or more GPs working in computerized, purpose-built surgeries, with facilities for disabled patients, nursing rooms, managers' offices, examination rooms and so on.

As well as the GPs, there are secretaries, managers, practice nurses, counsellors, psychiatric nurses, Macmillan nurses, social workers – a whole team of specialists working together to provide primary care, giving the required level of service to the patients.

Home visits are now seen as a routine part of the day, with local people coming out with every excuse under the sun for not actually getting to the surgery themselves. The worst one I experienced was of a mother who wanted her child to be seen by a doctor at 10.45 pm but who couldn't possibly get to the surgery where I was prepared to see her because her husband was down at the pub playing darts, which meant there would be no one left to look after the other kids in the house!

> **The general practice environment**
>
> - Smaller working environment, warm, supportive and friendly compared to hospitals.
> - Purpose-built facilities, with individual consulting rooms, fully computerized services and advanced diagnostic equipment.
> - GPs work as a part of the multidisciplinary team involved in primary healthcare provision.

The evolution of patients' notes

The way in which patients' notes are kept has gradually changed, from the bare minimum, to more comprehensive handwritten notes, to computerized notes in what are effectively paper-free practices. These notes now serve two purposes. First, the doctors are able to keep track of what they have done for their patients. Second, from a medico-legal point of view, they can protect doctors from law suits. Unfortunately, this country is gradually heading the same way that America has gone, where the legal implications of any decisions made about the care, treatment and management of a patient have to be considered.

Is the work limited?

The traditional view that all GPs do is see children with runny noses and sore throats is very outdated and, quite frankly, insulting. Many GPs have gained skills in minor surgery, some are actually fully skilled in other areas, such as accident and emergency or general surgery and can perform minor operations in local hospitals. Others act as clinical specialists working in conjunction with consultants in hospitals. GPs also work in conjunction with the Home Office to provide a health service to inmates in prisons, and to recently arrested people in police stations as police surgeons. Other GPs in rural areas can act as advanced life support providers and respond to '999' calls, getting to the scene of a major traffic accident or collapse of a patient before the arrival of the paramedics, who may have to drive some distance through traffic to get there. Also, practices now often have ECG machines to allow for the early diagnosis of heart arrythmias or heart attacks, and even ultrasound machines to reduce the need for prolonged waits for a hospital appointment to diagnose such things as gallstones. Some practices are even able to offer a service where the local consultants actually come to the practices on a monthly basis rather than the patients having to make their way to the hospitals.

Life beyond work

General practice is also still the career of choice for many doctors who decide that they want something else out of life apart from medicine. There are surprising numbers of posts on offer in the medical journals that are part-time, three-quarter time and full-time, with other options including participation in local on call teams of GPs called 'cooperatives'. Cooperatives have been introduced gradually over the last ten years and have drastically reduced the out-of-hours workload for GPs while also allowing them the freedom of being able to live as far away from their place of work as they reasonably wish to be. This kind of flexibility is attractive to women who wish to have children and doctors in general who wish to practise medicine but also indulge themselves in their other passions, such as music, crafts, arts or even politics.

Holding the purse strings

Money is, as ever, a dominant feature of life in the NHS, and general practice has had to take on board huge changes in work practices over the last two decades. We now have fundholding GPs who are essentially given an annual budget and told to do the best they can for their patients with that money. With the giving of control of the practices' money came the need to have practice managers who could organize the budgets and computer systems to keep track of where it was all going. Management costs spiralled and inequalities were highlighted between the practices that were and were not fundholding. Hospital consultants were not overly happy about the new power GPs were wielding regarding spending their money and so, now, after the system has finally been established, a new government comes along with new plans. No one knows if these plans will actually improve the situation, but what everyone does know is that a substantial amount of doctors' time and probably money will need to be given over to the installation of a new system.

Achieving quality

Just as there have been some scandalous reports of NHS money being wasted on the refurbishment of managers' offices or fancy training courses for them in five-star hotels, so sadly there have been occasional reports of below-standard GPs' malpractice, and bringing the profession into disrepute. These problems are being addressed with the introduction of harder exams to qualify for general practice, and also the possible introduction of five-yearly assessments for GPs to ensure that they are practising medicine at a high level of quality.

Not surprisingly, many GPs are concerned about the implications of such assessment. This is not because they are worried about their own individual competence, but, rather, because regular assessments will increase the level of stress in an already highly demanding job. They will be another burden on already limited spare time and will force GPs, yet again, to have to compromise the time spent with patients in favour of the bureaucracy of the job.

Furthermore, it is almost impossible anyway for an individual GP to work continuously at a substandard level. This is because almost all GPs work within a practice with several other partners, all of whom cover for each other's patients when holidays or sick leave are taken. The sharing of these patients allows GPs within a practice to see what each other is doing and, hence, any weaknesses within a practice are rapidly identified. All practices are also required to conduct internal audits on patient management and, in a way, there is a form of ongoing internal review and assessment within a practice, which helps maintain the high standards seen within the profession.

A key word in the 1990s has been 'burnout'. GPs were overwhelmed by the demands of the new system of fundholding and missed out on their personal time. General practice is a stressful career – one lapse in concentration can result in a patient leaving a consulting room with a prescription for indigestion when, in fact, they should be given something for their angina. Time will tell whether or not the White Paper will make equivalent demands to those that came with fundholding, bringing about a further spate of early retirements, which have so greatly contributed to the current national shortage of GPs.

Challenges and opportunities for GPs

- General practice offers opportunities for part-time work.
- General practice provides an excellent opportunity to work in other medical fields as well.
- GPs are challenged to keep in touch with modern medical treatments and advances.
- GPs are expected to deal with reforms and demands of the government of the day.

Summary

- General practice is a dynamic and exciting field of medicine, where technical advances, skills, knowledge and opportunities abound for doctors who wish to be able to express themselves in an environment rich in opportunities.
- Most doctors working in general practice thrive on the friendly and warm environment and see it as one of the major benefits when compared to the larger and more impersonal surroundings of a hospital.
- If politicians were to recognize that what GPs want is a period of stability rather than continual reform, then GPs would have the chance to settle down and concentrate on their patients again, rather than on new mountains of paperwork. We will have to wait and see which it is to be!

7

What is being a consultant like?

I remember watching one of the *Doctor in the House* films a few years ago and giggling with my friends at all the goings on, but, in particular, enjoying the masterfully commanding performance of the eminent consultant, Sir Lancelot Spratt. There is one classic moment when he catches a medical student off guard during a ward round. 'What's the bleeding time?', snarls Sir Lancelot, referring to the anticoagulation of a patient. 'Half past ten?', comes the reply. Sir Lancelot is not impressed!

Consultants are widely represented in all kinds of TV programmes – from the smooth, cool, desirable and sought-after men in *Casualty* to the corrupt or inept in *Cardiac Arrest*. In *ER*, they are all highly opinionated and unforgiving, while in *Doctor in the House* he was just plain terrifying. In other words, they come in all shapes and sizes, and it would be impossible and definitely foolhardy of me to try and describe what a 'typical' consultant is like.

Exactly the same principles apply when trying to describe what a consultant's job and lifestyle are like. It has been possible to make generalizations about the lifestyle and work of junior doctors because, in reality, these hospital jobs are all fairly consistent in their duration and content throughout the country. I cannot and dare not try to extend this principle into the consultant role, however. There is too much variation between consultants within a department, between one specialty and another and from hospital to hospital, region to region around the country.

The main features of being a consultant

It seems really strange that trying to define the workload and content of a consultant's job is so difficult. There are, however, some basic things that all consultants seem to have in common.

- All consultants are expected to work to a standard that satisfies the hospital's, region's, GPs' and patients' expectations and demands. This may be measured in parameters such as the number of operations performed or the number of patients seen in out-patient departments per year, with particular emphasis being placed on keeping hospital waiting lists as low as possible.
- Consultants try to perform this work within agreed departmental financial restrictions. When the money runs out, the department will grind to a halt or go over budget. This could, in effect, mean that a consultant trained to do procedures such as endoscopies may find that the department doesn't have the money to employ the theatre staff required to carry out the procedure. Hence, the endoscopy lists are cancelled, waiting lists grow, managers, GPs and patients are annoyed and consultants become frustrated.
- Consultants are expected to provide teaching to their juniors on a regular basis. This is the best way for the juniors to learn and, of course, the better trained the junior staff become, the more work they are able to do for their consultants.
- Many consultants will do research work. This is on top of the audit work that all departments are expected to conduct, and allows the consultants an opportunity to pursue particular interests in the field of their choice. This research work may end up being submitted to the relevant specialist medical journals and, hence, being published nationally and internationally. Some research will actually end up changing procedures done nationally and even internationally. Sometimes this leads to consultants being invited to conferences at home or abroad, giving speeches to eminent colleagues on their latest findings. These conferences can be quite good fun and are often sponsored by a medical company with flights, food, accommodation and drinks all for free.

- Consultants need to stay at the forefront of knowledge in their chosen specialty. That, after all, is the whole idea of specializing – to become a specialist in one particular, small area of the huge world of medicine. Skills will need to be practised and modernized, and any new techniques or medical principles will have to reviewed and introduced to the hospital under the guidance of the consultant. This will inevitably include a review of the financial implications of such new introductions and, hence, one consultant may find that they are in competition with other colleagues for the necessary money as they wish to introduce new schemes of their own.
- Consultants have to provide emergency 24-hour cover to patients, just as the juniors and GPs have to do. And, just like the juniors, this is usually based on an on call rota. Although, thankfully, the frequency of callouts in the middle of the night lessens as you climb the hospital ladder, nevertheless it remains a burden and restriction on consultants' lifestyles as you have to remain available, uncommitted and sober on a regular basis for the occasional emergency.
- Consultants work in a variety of environments. Most will be the named consultant of, effectively, their own ward, where their patients will be admitted and looked after by their own team of doctors and nurses, who will attempt to care for those patients in line with the consultant's medical preferences for treatment. We have all come across the twice-weekly consultant-led ward round, the showpiece for the ward, where the patients are presented to the consultant with all their juniors present, as a team, *en masse*, with senior nursing staff and ancillary staff often accompanying the show.

For the rest of the working week, consultants run regular outpatient clinics, often in both the main hospital and community hospitals and now even in GPs' surgeries. There will be operating lists for surgeons, endoscopy lists for gastroenterologists, invasive procedure lists for radiologists, cardiac angiogram lists for cardiologists. There will be lectures to all grades of staff within the local health authority, from medical students to the GPs, interview panels to sit in on, managerial meetings to fit in, inevitable paperwork ... and *more* paperwork. The list of options and possibilities goes on and on.

The financial aspects

Consultants in certain specialties have considerable earning potential in the private healthcare sector. This may be on top of the normal full-time NHS commitment or, the choice of many consultants, working slightly less than full-time for the NHS and devoting a proportion of the working week to the private sector. The reasons for this are obvious – the money that can be earned for a private consultation or for performing private operations can, in the most extreme cases, make the NHS salary look like mere pocket money.

Many doctors see this as the only way to boost their income to a level that seems appropriate to the hours, training, effort and responsibility that the career demands. However, I know that many members of the public feel it is becoming a world of the 'haves' and 'have nots' where medical services are concerned, and that consultants who have been trained within the NHS shouldn't be allowed to do private work. Nevertheless, the reality of the situation is that if the public still wants highly intelligent and dedicated people to enter the medical profession, then it has got to accept that it is necessary for consultants to be able to achieve a decent income. The alternative is that Britain's top doctors will leave this country, as evidenced by the computer 'brain drain'.

Typically, a consultant will be given their post some time around the age of 35, and keep that post for the rest of their working life. Most consultants aim to retire in their late 50s or very early 60s, depending on the state of their finances and physical well-being.

How much does a consultant earn? That's like asking 'How long is a piece of string?' It is fairly irrelevant to give an actual figure, because, within six months of the book being published, the figures will be out of date. Suffice to say that most consultants command an NHS income equal to that of GPs, a decent solicitor or very similar to a headteacher of one of the largest state schools. Comparisons with private-sector managers are difficult as most of these careers include contract bonuses, company cars, weighty retirement packages and so on. However, there is tremendous job stability – illness is unlikely to go out of fashion, so the need for doctors is set to continue!

The future?

Just as the chapter on general practitioners was deliberately brief, so is this one. The reason is that if you happen to be 17 years old and are reading this book with a view to becoming a doctor and, ultimately, a consultant, then you've got around 15 years to go before you will reach the level required to be a consultant. Who knows what on earth the job will have become by then? Will the NHS, as we know it now, still exist then? Will the somewhat historical title of 'consultant' have been replaced with something more in line with the twenty-first century – perhaps you could be retitled 'senior specialist' or even 'managing medical specialist practitioner'.

The possibilities for the future are huge and exciting. New diseases are always appearing, treatments being developed, diagnostic equipment coming on line, operations being attempted. The consultants are the ones at the forefront of this process, the ones who will see in the new and replace the old and carry the responsibility of providing the best specialist treatment for us all in years to come.

Summary

- The basics are unlikely to change in the near future. That is, doctors will continue to work their way up the ladder, from house officer all the way to consultant, becoming highly specialized *en route*, and then spend the rest of their careers as experts in their chosen field.
- The workload doesn't necessarily ease as the ladder is climbed, but the nature of the work changes and the ability to indulge in a particular interest and then become an expert in that interest is one of the great attractions of the job.
- The challenges of the job are those of maintaining that specialist knowledge so that it is always at the most modern and highest level, to pass that knowledge on to the juniors and to use it to the benefit of patients. After all, that is what it's all about in the end.

8

What is it like being a woman in medicine?

For this chapter, I owe massive thanks to a great friend and professional colleague, Dr Beth de Sousa, a qualified GP and mother of a gorgeous baby! Thanks, and over to you.

When Dave asked me to give a woman's perspective on medicine, my initial reaction was to ask 'Why distinguish between the two sexes?' After all, we both do exactly the same job.

Yes, it's true that we both carry stethoscopes, but, like it or not, we are different and no matter how subtle those differences, they influence the way we work.

The statistics

Traditionally, there have been far fewer females than males in the medical profession. Over the last 30 years, however, there has been a dramatic change so that now almost all medical schools have an equal intake of males and females. However, despite this, only 15.5 per cent of hospital consultants are female and women only account for 25.9 per cent of GP principals.

So, why should we be encouraging women to go into medicine? Obviously, for all the reasons that men give, but also because, undeniably, we make great doctors.

To expand a little:

- Women are used to juggling the various demands of family life and so tend to be very organized, very able to cope with multiple problems simultaneously and be good, broad thinkers.
- Women can bring a personal understanding of and empathy with 'women's problems' to a consultation and, similarly, when working with children.
- Some people simply prefer talking to a woman.

Why aren't there more women in medicine?

There are several reasons for this.

- First and foremost, family. It isn't that the family is the be all and end all in our lives, it's just that the system as it stands makes it very difficult, in some areas, for us to do a job that, as Dave has said, is more than just a job. It is, or can be, an all-consuming way of life. Traditionally, if a man had to move about the country with his work, the woman, who in most households earned less, would follow. Especially in such a nomadic profession as medicine, this can create difficulties if the man also has an established career in one place and is unable to move. The result, often, is long periods of separation.
- Being pregnant while working can be physically very demanding. A friend tells a story of how, when she was on call over a 24-hour period while she was working in hospital, she wore a pedometer to measure how far she walked during that time. She clocked up 17.5 miles! That total didn't take into account anything she did once she actually stood still to do some work. Securing a job while pregnant can also be difficult. Although unquestionably illegal, an employer who is faced with two job applicants of equal calibre will choose the one who isn't pregnant because the last thing they want is for their house officer to go off on maternity leave halfway through a job, leaving them with the prospect of having to fill the position with expensive locums.

- The speed of change in medicine is so rapid that taking a break for maternity leave can lead to a real loss of confidence. As yet, there are no return to work packages like those found in so many other professions.
- Many women feel that they want to devote a large chunk of time to their family while their kids are young and, consequently, don't want to go back to full-time work. Career advice is poor and, until recently, there were very few good part-time packages. More of that later.

There are other barriers as well.

Medicine is still a very male-dominated profession in some areas, such as surgery, that has been renowned in the past for cultivating sexism. This can be both antagonistic to a relaxed atmosphere at work and also to the progression of a career path.

In general practice, where you may be working closely with the same small group of people over a number of years, there has to be give and take. Women who have young families may find it much more difficult to be as flexible as is required in some practices *and* find good childcare, pick up and take kids to school and drop everything when a child is ill. It's a very delicate balancing act, which most women find difficult to get right. Colleagues need to have an understanding of the situation, but such understanding is not always forthcoming.

Until recently, in male-dominated specialties such as surgery, it was not uncommon to find that women consultants had not had children. Either they had made that sacrifice for the sake of their career or perhaps they had found it easier to get on in that area because they had no desire to have children anyway. A specialty such as this requires you to give your all, to the exclusion of everything else.

Women working in fields such as general practice have found that female patients tend to gravitate towards them, particularly if they have a 'women's problem'. In a practice, where there are only one or two female doctors (this is the norm in my area, East Devon, where there are only two full-time female doctors in the whole area), this means that female doctors' lists may consist predominantly of gynaecological problems. These can be more time-consuming, the work can then become monotonous (the doctors are no longer in 'general' practice in the true sense of the word) and the effect can be that the doctors become deskilled in other areas.

Positive changes

You will be pleased to hear that these things are changing. With a larger body of women in the profession year by year, we have a greater voice. This, in turn, is starting to lead to the availability of a greater variety of options.

Over the last few years, especially in general practice, a huge change in the work ethic has taken place. When my father started in general practice, the norm was single-handed or two-man practices providing 24 hours a day, 7 days per week cover. That meant that, in reality, if you were a single-handed practice, you were working non-stop. Now the norm is for larger practices so that the workload is distributed more thinly, but also the ethic that 'work is paramount, over all other aspects of life' is disappearing.

That is not to say that doctors are no longer dedicated to providing the best service for their patients – it has always been the case and, I hope, will remain so. Rather, there is now the realization that the best care is not given when you have not slept the night before because you were out on call. Also, that you have a lot more to give to patients if you are able to talk to them like a normal human being and, surely, to be able to do that you must be living a 'normal' lifestyle. It is the realization that if you are burnt out at the age of 40 as a result of overwork and stress, your patients are not getting the best deal.

Part-time working

One of the catalysts of change has been women who have wanted to combine having a family with work and introduced the concept of part-time partners. Just 30 years ago, it was unheard of for men to be working part-time. In 1991, the government introduced major changes into the health system, the effect of which was a dramatic increase in GPs' workloads. Stress at work correspondingly increased and the word 'burnout' started to become a familiar part of general practice vocabulary. As it became more acceptable for women to work part-time, some of the men started to try it as a means of self-preservation and discovered what a fantastic option it had the potential to be.

Since then, many more part-time packages have become available in general practice, and the hospital system is starting to catch on as well. However, a lot of the packages have been criticized for their poor pay, poor postgraduate teaching opportunities and lack of voice in the workplace. Also, part-time training posts can mean it takes forever to complete the training. It is still the case in hospitals that a part-time job has to be created and funded by the health authority in addition to the normal quota of jobs in a particular department, as there are few or no part-time training posts.

This situation is changing and there is the promise of better things to come. A lot of women find part-time work an extremely attractive and enjoyable way in which to continue their careers. If you are lucky, a part-time job can pay extremely well, allow for flexibility in terms of hours, give you self-confidence and enable you to keep your hand in as preparation for the time when you may want to increase your commitment.

The kinds of changes that will draw women back into medicine

- Better part-time packages.
- Improved hours of work in hospital jobs.
- A more substantial voice in the workplace.
- Out-of-hours packages that allow a decrease in the on call commitment.

Overnight working

Night-time work was one of the major causes of women not wanting to carry on in medicine. There was not only the onerous workload, but also the very real danger of being assaulted when visiting patients' homes in the middle of the night, especially in some of the bigger cities. A friend of mine starting her first term in her first year at medical school spent a night on call with an anaesthetist friend to see what it was like. She left medical school soon after. She knew that she would be unable to cope with that sort of stress. Being up at night, all night, and having the responsibility of patients' lives in your hands when all you can think about is how much you long for your bed, is very hard. Done regularly it's bad. Done regularly until you're 60 it's many times worse.

There is good news! Hospital hours have been dramatically reduced over the past five years, and similarly, in general practice, the introduction of the 'night-time cooperative service' has greatly reduced the burdens of providing medical services to patients overnight.

Summary

- The health service of 50 years ago is unrecognizable to us now. I have hope that things will continue to improve for women in medicine.
- There can be few other jobs that offer such enormous job satisfaction, the chance to make a difference to people's lives every day, good pay, unquestionable job security and the potential to work exactly the number of hours you want to work. That to me is the ideal job description.

9

What are the financial aspects of being a doctor?

It is typically British, but among many classes of society, and in particular the middle classes, it is still considered rude to talk openly about what you are paid. Medicine remains one of these establishments where, give or take a bit, most of us have a fair idea of what the other is earning, but it is still rarely talked about openly. To me, having a career serves two purposes. First, it provides job satisfaction and, second, it enables me to bring home an income. So, to write a book about careers in medicine without mentioning the financial aspects may be politically correct, but it would be wholly unfair to you.

I mentioned earlier that, in theory, anyone can leave school aged 16, go straight to work as an unskilled something or other and gradually work their way up the ladder until they are earning good money. Indeed, many people have done this over the years and still continue to do so. Medicine, however, is different. Anyone beginning a medical career in the 1990s will spend five years accumulating debts and undoubtedly feel hard done by if they compare their situation to that of a person who went straight into work and is now in their own house, with a car, going on holidays and so on. However, the years of poverty are more than made up for in later life when GPs' and consultants' earnings will outstrip those of all but the most exceptionally gifted of the semiskilled.

At medical school

Two years of 'A' levels initially and then five years at medical school. It is an expensive time for everyone. Any student grant you may have got is all but gone, and fees of £1000 per year mean that, unless there are some wealthy and supportive parents around, the debts are going to mount.

A roof over your head

Typical student accommodation will cost anything from £30 to £60 per week, depending on the city you are in (London, of course, is the most expensive) and which area within the city you choose (the old, 'red light' areas of cities tend to be the cheapest areas to live, whereas accommodation within easy walking distance of the university is obviously more expensive).

Other expenses

Food and drink, clothes, the odd holiday, council tax, medical equipment (stethoscope, opthalmoscope), smarter clothes for ward work, transport to different hospitals – all add up to a surprisingly large total. The new student fees will also have a huge impact, especially given that the standard medical course is five years and many people sit a BSc year, taking the total to six years' study.

Sources of funds

Most medical students hold part-time jobs during term time and full-time holiday jobs in the first two years, during which the university year only accounts for 30 weeks, giving plenty of scope for holiday work. In the final three years, the term time expands, typically, to a 44-week year, giving little opportunity for those holiday jobs. The options for money include, perhaps, a student grant, bank loans and parent loans. Other options are to seek sponsorship from the armed forces, which will eventually necessitate a period of service with the chosen force in return for that sponsorship. As yet, there are virtually no offers of private sponsorship from companies, as, in reality, you would be pretty useless to them for at least another three years after you have qualified, assuming you decided to continue with medicine.

Being in debt

Debts are, therefore, unavoidable, and the extent of the debt will depend entirely on how you live your life as a student. For example, you could make the decision that this is the first time you've been free to do what you want to do and that you want to have fun while you're young and free of commitment, especially knowing how hard your future career is likely to be. Excessive partying, skiing holidays, summer holidays, a nice student house, a car and the odd meal out at a restaurant will easily leave you requiring £20,000. This is an average of £4000 per year, excluding the annual tuition fees of £1000 per year, so taking the grand total to over £25,000.

On the other hand, you could have a job in a local bar during term time and do holiday jobs in the breaks, still have a really good time and end up with debts of only £5000. It all depends on the individual, where you choose to study and what you're prepared to sacrifice during the training. I guess it also depends on family support, as this can make the biggest difference.

Whatever you do, the debts just seem to keep mounting. This is very scary, especially given that it is the first time many people will have had access to a bank account of their own. Nasty letters from the bank come thick and fast, and even more annoying are those ones that keep coming reminding you how overdrawn you are, and the charge of £10 for each of them. It used to drive us all round the bend! Don't worry, though – it's all just a bullying tactic from the banks. The reason the bank lends you the money in the first place is because it knows that, above all other students, it's the medics who will have a guaranteed job at the end of their training and probably for the rest of their lives. The debts, in effect, are a sure bet for the banks – they almost always get their money back from us, with interest, of course!

I guess what I'm saying is that the debts incurred as a medical student may seem daunting and offputting, especially if you will not get any financial support from your family, but, in the longer term, a doctor has the potential to be one of the highest paid people in the country. So, the student debts will, before long, seem like a distant memory. Added to that is the good name, respect and reputation that being a doctor still carries with it (unlike politicians, for example) and the almost guaranteed job-for-life comfort (again, unlike politicians).

Student reminders

- Try to stick to a budget – don't get carried away with it all.
- Try to stay afloat – get part-time jobs whenever you can.
- Don't be put off medicine by the thought of debt.
- Don't get stressed out by panicky bank managers.
- Think long term – remember what a great career medicine is.

The house year and the first contract

The house officer year comes as a great relief to everyone – students, parents and bank managers alike. It means to the students that you've finally made it, to the parents that they are finally free of their responsibilities to you and to the bank managers that you're not a dropout and will be able to repay the debts you've accrued.

What happens on your first day

How much do house officers earn? Well, as usual in the NHS, it is not always that simple. On your first day as a house officer you will be warmly welcomed to the hospital and probably given a quick set of talks on the first morning of work, before having lunch, collecting your bleeper and being set free to find the ward in which you will be based for the next six months. One of those talks will be from the personnel manager, and that person will probably be responsible for ensuring that you have signed a contract for the six-month post. You will soon discover that the terms and conditions of a doctor's contract are unique to our profession and will govern a junior doctor's lifestyle for several years to come.

Aspects of the contract to note

- Among the joys of the contract will be a clause stating that you have a duty to cover the hospital in all eventualities. Thus, should someone go off sick suddenly, the hospital can insist that you cover that person's workload and on call commitments, even if that means being called out of bed in the middle of the night, missing a weekend off work with only a few hours' notice or even having to cancel holiday plans at the last minute.
- Another big joy is trying to come to terms with the pay structure, which consists of standard working hours and additional duty hours (ADHs). A typical hospital contract will be for a standard 40-hour working week, covering the usual 9 to 5 working day for the 5 days of Monday to Friday. All extra hours worked – namely the hours on call overnight during the week and all the hours over a weekend, are the ADHs. The number of ADHs agreed in your contract will be directly related to how many nights your job demands you to be on call per week. Therefore, a 1:4 rota (working every fourth night and every fourth weekend) will have more ADHs than a 1:6.
- The other aspect of ADHs is that they are paid at a level that is supposed to reflect the intensity of that on call work. Hence, a job that is accepted to be quiet during the nights, with minimal work requirement, will pay what is called Class III ADHs – a pay scale for which every ADH pays only 50 per cent of a standard working hour. In other words, if your standard contract pays at a rate of £8 per hour, the Class III ADH will earn you £4 per hour. A more labour-intensive on call, where the doctor can expect to be working most of the time, although with the possibility of some rest periods, will pay out at Class II ADHs. Here

each ADH pays at 70 per cent of basic pay. A fully intensive job with no possibility of rest will pay at Class I ADHs, which is in fact the full 100 per cent of normal salary.
- Another aspect is the option to pay into the NHS pension scheme, known as the superannuation scheme. This is the State-run scheme, universally offered by all hospitals to all doctors, to which almost every doctor chooses to contribute from day one of their working lives. The finer details aside, essentially, for every pound you pay into the scheme, the NHS adds a bit extra on top and, then, when you come to retire, you get a big cheque and a pension for the rest of your life. The basic idea is to pay a total of 40 years' worth of superannuation, and if you retire on 40 years of payments, then you get your full pension. If, however, you only work for 35 years, then you get less. Clever people will only work for 35 years, but pay additional voluntary contributions (AVCs) to take their total to the equivalent of 40 years. This enables them to retire early, but still receive a full pension. In this respect, the scheme is both flexible and generous, which is why you will be encouraged to contribute to it and why nearly all doctors do.

The contents of a contract

- Junior contracts are almost always offered for a six-month period only.
- The standard is a 40-hour week, with additional duty hours on top.
- ADHs should be paid at Class I, II or III, depending on job workload.
- ADHs are, in fact, paid at a level that is set by what the hospital can afford.
- Standard deductions include payments into the superannuation scheme.

In practice, almost all house officer contracts pay the standard 40 hours per week, then up to 32 ADHs for a typical 1:5 job, which will be paid at Class III level. That works out to be 56 fully paid hours per week, although you will, of course, be working the 72 hours stated in the contract.

Unfortunately, the NHS is a perennially penniless institution and so the level of the ADHs in no way reflects the workload of your on call time. Although, according to the rules, you should be guaranteed something like six hours of uninterrupted rest during a night you are on call and being paid Class III ADHs, in fact you will probably get to bed for about a third of that time. In effect, you should be paid at Class II rates, but this would of course cost the hospital more money and hospitals don't like that. The managers know that most house officers are scared and unwilling to stand up and complain as they need a good reference at the end of each job. Unfortunately many consultants don't really care about their juniors' pay either, offering a job at Class III rates and letting it stay that way.

So what does it all add up to? Friends of mine, in 1997–98, as house officers are taking home around £1200 per month, after deductions. Not a fortune by any standards, particularly given the number of hours worked for it. However, it is still more than many people earn, with the gross annual income probably already exceeding the general population's national average. In the first month of being a house officer, you jump from social class five to a doctor in social class one!

And after house year?

After house year, the general rule of thumb is that every time you jump a grade – say, from house officer to SHO or from SHO to registrar – your salary takes a little jump. Then, for every year you work in the NHS at that grade, your pay will increase by roughly £100 per month. So, for example, a first-year SHO may take home £1400 per month, while a third-year SHO will take home around £1600. Otherwise, the same rules as above still apply, with the number of ADHs and their Class, being the determining factors in the final calculations.

Consultants and GPs

Call it a cop out, call me 'chicken' or just suggest I value my career too much to compromise it by attempting to suggest how much GPs and consultants earn. The plain truth is that there are too many variables to allow me to make any more than basic suggestions.

GPs are normally employed by their local/regional health authority. The salary each receives is dependent on a multitude of things, including of course whether you are full-time or part-time, your total years of service, whether or not your practice achieves all its targets, whether your practice is fundholding or non-fundholding what extra services your practice lays on for the local population (such as minor surgery) whether or not the practice is self-dispensing or not (that is, if it does or does not have a pharmacy on site) ... the list goes on and on.

Private work is, on the whole, extremely limited in general practice, although as soon as there is a demand for it from the general public, I'm sure there will be GPs who will be prepared to offer the desired services. Having said that, the current national average net remuneration for an NHS GP is around £45,000 per year.

Consultants are still employed, in general, by the hospitals, and, again, are paid according to whether they are full- or part-time. The number of years of service makes an extra difference, just as it does for the juniors. The availability and desire to do private work creates the greatest differences at present between the consultants (where there is a thriving private sector) and the GPs (where, at present, there is not). There is little doubt about the earning potential of doing work in the private sector. A successful surgeon with a healthy private practice can earn enough privately to be able to treat the NHS pay as little more than pocket money.

In this respect, the earnings potential of medicine can more than match that of almost all other careers. The fact is, however, it is always the exceptional earners who catch the headlines. For every top-flight barrister earning hundreds of thousands per year in high-profile cases in London, you'll find a doctor earning equivalent amounts of money. On the other hand, for every 'average'-earning city solicitor, you'll find an equally 'average' GP or consultant. If it's money you want, then a career in medicine has the potential to provide it, depending what field of medicine you choose and how hard you're prepared to work for it.

Outgoings and expenses

There are lots of societies and memberships that doctors need to maintain from the start of their careers and unfortunately the cost of these comes out of our salaries. For instance, no doctor can practise without their General Medical Council certificate, for which there is an annual fee. Also, legal protection against prosecution from angry, or plain mad, patients is a necessity. There are several special medico-legal protection companies serving doctors of all grades, such as the Medical Defence Union (MDU) and Medical Protection Society (MPS), and, again, an annual fee applies. It is wise to be a member of your chosen specialty's college, which also costs a certain amount per year. Most doctors, at least initially anyway, will wish to be a member of the British Medical Association (BMA) and, for this too, there is a fee. All junior doctors have to pay to sit their examinations and then, ironically, as we saw earlier, have to buy their certificates once they've passed those exams. Most juniors pay a monthly contribution towards the running of the doctors' mess within a hospital . . . and so it goes on.

Fortunately, doctors also become very good at reclaiming expenses from the Inland Revenue! A recent article commented on how, within reason, it was possible for a GP to reclaim against his taxes the costs of courses, conferences, books, magazines, medical subscriptions, cleaning and laundry expenses, some telephone bills, even home security and pet dogs (which of course double as guard dogs). If you ever get bored with medicine, you can always walk straight into an accountancy job!

Summary

- Medicine is a strange career, financially speaking. You start off in debt, then work long hours as a junior, then pay seemingly extortionate fees to sit exams and receive a certificate to show you've passed. After a training period that, in total, encompasses at least 13 years, you can become a consultant. At this point, depending on which specialty you have chosen and if your principles will allow it, you will earn, at the least, a healthy middle-class income or, at best, an obscene amount of money!
- A minimum of nine years' training is required to become a GP, at which stage, again, the earnings equate with those of other decent middle-class professions, although, as yet, the chances of accruing substantial earnings from private work remain slim. All this may yet change as the NHS evolves over the next decade.
- Whatever else, don't be put off medicine just because of the student debts – they are a short-term concern within a 40-year career. The thought of these debts should serve to focus your mind and make you think carefully about a career in medicine, but should not be considered a reason to abandon thoughts of entering this excellent career.

10

Are there other options within medicine?

Medicine can offer gateways to careers not only as traditional doctors, be they consultants or GPs, but also to other careers encompassing almost every walk of life.

Many students at university spend three years doing non-vocational courses in subjects such as geography, English, politics and so on and never actually become an English teacher or politician or whatever. Likewise, there is nothing to stop a medical student from completing their five years at medical school and then using their medical degree to do something completely different.

Using your skills in different ways

Equally, if a medical student chooses to continue after finals and become a doctor, they still do not have to practise. At this point, further opportunities become available. Doctors are sought after to give medical opinions on TV shows, write books or for medical pages in national newspapers.

Alternatively, doctors are employed in all the armed services and are required by the police and prison services, public health services, community medicine and occupational health. Many doctors also choose to work for charities or set-ups aimed at helping the underprivileged in other countries – Médecins sans Frontières being a classic example of this. Doctors working for such groups go to foreign, sometimes war-torn, countries where poverty-stricken and starved populations urgently require the input of medical teams.

Doctors are also required by specialist sports institutions, to help in the preparation and maintain the well-being of people on expeditions around the world, for climbing, diving, skiing, mountaineering and so on. Doctors are required to be present at major sporting events from rugby games to boxing. Doctors may also find themselves being employed by sports teams to provide specialist care for their athletes.

Doctors can also take on the full-time role of organizing and overviewing the training of future doctors. This could be done by becoming, for example, a dean of medicine within a medical school or even a regional dean, responsible for watching over the training of junior doctors within a local county. Doctors are also needed to work within the medical institutions themselves – the British Medical Association, for example.

Doctors can use their respected position in society to help establish themselves in other careers, such as politics, and several famous doctors spring to mind who have become top politicians in recent years.

Summary

- As can be seen, there is, in fact, hardly a single area of industry or commerce that *doesn't* have a role for doctors.
- Choosing to do a medical degree at university, therefore, opens as many doors as some might think it closes, and it takes only a little effort and a sense of adventure to broaden your horizons and go for something a bit more original than the standard career path.
- The opportunities are there if you are prepared to take them.

11

Decision time

When I went for that first interview at medical school and said that the reason I wanted to be a doctor was so that I could help people, I said it partly from honesty and partly from naivety and ignorance. *Everyone* involved in the health profession wants to help people and see them get better, and there are many ways of participating in this process, from cleaning the operating theatres to ensure they are aseptic, to performing the operations themselves. Each person involved is reliant on the other in an integrated way. A top orthopaedic surgeon may rebuild a shattered limb, but it will be the physiotherapists who get the patient walking again. A GP may diagnose and medically treat a stroke patient, but it will be the occupational therapists who will ensure that the person develops the skills required to enable them to continue to live an independent life. Doctors may be the ones to diagnose a rare illness, but often it is the nurses on the ward and in the community who provide the personal care required to keep that person healthy on a day-to-day basis. All these professionals, plus many others, work together to help people, and each is as important as the next.

To become a doctor requires huge commitment, and you have to be prepared to sacrifice your personal time and life to a level that few other careers demand. It is about being able to take responsibility for what you do. It is about making more decisions in a day than many people make in a month. It is about being adaptable, broad-minded and non-judgemental about those you are trying to help. It is about being a key member of a team and being able to work within a team to the harmonious benefit of all. It is also about staying in touch with the views, fears and expectations of the public, the demands of government and the needs of your community. It is about being able to communicate with people who may be afraid, distrustful and even resentful, but who still need your help.

Furthermore, becoming a doctor requires an acceptance of the fact that the career you think you're getting yourself into now will probably be very different in 20 years' time. Medicine is one of the most exciting careers in terms of progression – consultants may be retitled, job descriptions changed, examinations reviewed, training structures altered, current illnesses cured and new illnesses discovered, technologies replaced and updated. The NHS, as it currently stands, has changed almost completely from the way it was 20 years ago, and so we should expect the same to happen in a further 20 years' time.

Whatever the job structure, though, the basic necessities a doctor requires will probably remain the same. Being prepared to make sacrifices, be a team player and so on are all important, and will help any doctor be a successful one. If you can do all these things and remain compassionate and caring at the same time, then the chances are that you'll find medicine the most rewarding of all careers. Medicine is an honourable and worthy career that is sometimes frustrating, but ultimately stimulating and heartwarming, always surprising, often satisfying and addictively interesting. That's why we do it and that's why there's so much competition to get into medical school.

If you've read this book from beginning to end, you'll now have a pretty good idea of what a career in medicine is all about. To keep the book brief, there are many generalizations, many areas only lightly touched on that deserve full chapters in themselves, but, hopefully, you will have gained enough of an insight into the career structure, the effects on your lifestyle, the exams, commitments, upheavals and stresses. You will also have gained an idea as to why we all do it – the satisfaction of being part of a great profession, social respect, guaranteed employment, opportunities and stimulation of the work itself.

So now we are back to where we started, and I shall finish by leaving you to answer the simple question we started with –

'So you want to be a doctor?'